THE POETRY

OF W. B. YEATS

by

Yvor Winters

THE SWALLOW PAMPHLETS NUMBER 10

ALAN SWALLOW, *Denver*

Copyright 1960 by Yvor Winters

Library of Congress Catalog Card Number: 60-14593

I

We have been told many times that we do not have to take the ideas of Yeats seriously in order to appreciate his poetry; but if this is true, Yeats is the first poet of whom it has ever been true. We need to understand the ideas of Donne and of Shakespeare in order to appreciate their works, and we have to take their ideas seriously in one sense or another, and it is possible to take their ideas seriously much of the time. A great deal of scholarly work has been done on their ideas, and some of this work has contributed to our appreciation of what they wrote. A great deal of scholarly work has been done on Yeats in recent years; unfortunately, the better one understands him, the harder it is to take him seriously.*

I shall refer rather often in this essay to a recent book by John Unterecker[1]. The book gives a more detailed account than any other which I know of what Yeats was doing or thought he was doing. It accepts without question Yeats's ideas regarding the nature of poetry, ideas which in my opinion are unacceptable. And like almost every other publication on Yeats it accepts without question the notion that Yeats was a very great poet and it merely substitutes exegesis for criticism. For example, Mr. Unterecker explains the meaning of an early poem, *The Two Trees,* (p. 47) and I think correctly. Then, with no explanation whatever, he refers to it as "so grand a poem." The poem is obviously a bad poem: it is sentimental and stereotyped at every point. Mr. Unterecker is a split personality: on the one hand he is a careful scholar and on the other he is a critic with neither talent nor training. In this he resembles most of the literary scholars with whose work I am ac-

---

* In this essay I shall discuss a good many of Yeats's poems in detail. It is impractical to quote them in full. After the title of each poem discussed, therefore, I shall give the page number of the *The Collected Poems of W. B. Yeats,* The Macmillan Co., New York, 1951.

3

quainted, but his book is very helpful notwithstanding.

Mr. Unterecker says (*A Reader's Guide*, p. 23), and I believe correctly so far as Yeats's theory goes: "Because all occult symbols linked ultimately to a universal harmony, any consistent intrepretatation of one of them was 'right' since it in turn led to that harmony. The only danger, as Yeats frequently pointed out, is that the reader is likely to limit the symbol's meaning and so throw it into the area of allegory." For some readers, this passage may call for brief explanation. In terms of medieval poetry, the word *symbol* refers to an object which has a one-to-one relationship to a meaning: that is, the whale is Satan, and Dante's panther, lion and wolf are lust, pride, and avarice. When such symbols occur in the action of a narrative, we have allegory. But Yeats employs the word *symbol* as we employ it in speaking of French symbolist poetry, and the meaning of the term is reversed. Mallarmé was the great theorist of this kind of thing: his aim was to produce a kind of poetic absolute in which rational meaning would be as far as possible suppressed and suggestion would be isolated. He was not wholly successful in his aim, for many—perhaps most—of his later poems appear to deal, as obscurely as possible, with the theory of this kind of poetry; but he tried. In so far as this kind of effort succeeds, we have, in the very words of the Master, an "aboli bibelot d'inanité sonore." This is what Frank Kermode calls the romantic image[2], that is, the image which is meaningless, inscrutable, the image of which the dancer with the beautiful body and the expressionless face is the perfect

type. Kermode disapproves of the method and he finds it in Yeats, but he is overcome by Yeats and considers him a great poet notwithstanding. What Yeats and Mr. Unterecker mean by a "universal harmony" it would be hard to say. Mr. Unterecker says elsewhere (*A Reader's Guide*, p. 34).

Any analogy we can construct for the symbol, any meaning we assign to it, is legitimate so long as we recognize that that meaning is *not* its meaning. Its meaning must always be more elusive than any value we can—with words—fix to it. All that the meaning we assign to a symbol can ever be is either part of its meaning or one of its possible meanings. No symbol has a meaning.

And again (*A Reader's Guide*, p. 40) he tells us that the symbol does not give us meaning "but instead the feeling of meaning . . . an undefined sense of order, or rightness, of congruence at the heart of things." I discussed this theory of the feeling of meaning a good many years ago in writing of what I called pseudo-reference and a little later in my essay on Poe. And Mr. Unterecker again: "Yeats allows us to experience . . . the necessary if momentary illusions of order which give us courage to live." Foolish as these ideas may seem, they are, as nearly as I can make out, Yeats's ideas as well as Mr. Unterecker's, and they are commonly accepted in our time.

Yeats, of course, often deviated from this theory of the symbol and wrote forthright poems; and he often wrote in symbols more nearly akin to medieval symbols than to Mallarméan. But the theory provides a dark and convenient little corner into which the apologist may retreat rapidly backward whenever he is embarrassed by the meaning.

4

I will try to summarize the principal ideas which motivate Yeats's poetry. All good comes from the emotions, and even madness is good. *Wisdom* is a pejorative term; *ignorance* is the reverse. In Yeats's later work *lust* and *rage* become increasingly prominent and they represent virtues. Sexual union is equated with the mystical experience or at least participates in the mystical experience in a literal way. This is not the same thing as the analogy of sexual union which is sometimes used by the Christian mystics. The Christian mystics tell us that the mystical experience is absolutely different from any human experience and thus cannot be described in language, but that the experience can be suggested by analogy. This leads, I think, to a more or less fraudulent poetry, for the poet is dealing with an ineffable experience by dealing with something irrelevant to it; but the fraud is, in a sense, an honest one, for the rules of the procedure are known. But for Yeats the two experiences are of the same kind, the only difference being that the sexual experience is less nearly pure than would be the experience of disembodied spirits: we are given the pure experience in *Ribh at the Tomb of Baile and Ailinn*, in which Ribh reads his book by the pure light given off by the orgasm of the disembodied lovers.

Yeats's concept of what would be the ideal society is also important. Such a society would be essentially agrarian, with as few politicians and tradesmen as possible. The dominant class would be the landed gentry; the peasants would also be important, but would stay in their place; a fair sprinkling of beggars (some of

them mad), of drunkards, and of priests would make the countryside more picturesque. The gentlemen should be violent and bitter, patrons of the arts, and the maintainers of order; they should be good horsemen, preferably reckless horseman (if the two kinds may exist in one); and they should be fond of fishing. The ladies should be beautiful and charming, should be gracious hostesses (although there is a place for more violent ladies—videlicet Mrs. French in *The Tower*), should if possible be musicians, should drive men mad, love, marry, and produce children, should not be interested in ideas, and should ride horseback, preferably to hounds. So far as I can recollect, the ladies are not required to go fishing. What Yeats would have liked would have been an eighteenth-century Ireland of his own imagining. He disliked the political and argumentative turmoil of revolutionary Ireland; he would scarcely have thought that the order which has emerged was sufficiently picturesque to produce poetry.

Yeats's cosmological and psychological system has been so fully discussed by others that I shall merely summarize it. He believed that history proceeds through cycles of two thousand years each. Every cycle begins in a state of objectivity (which is evil) and with violence; it proceeds through subjectivity (which is good), through pure subjectivity (which is too much of a good thing), and it then proceeds toward objectivity and ultimate dispersal and a new beginning. The life of every human goes through a similar cycle. Yeats had two diagrams for this process: the diagram of the phases of the moon and the diagram of the interpenetratıng cones (gyres, pernes, or spindles). The first of these is a circle with the twenty-eight phases of the moon marked upon it. At the top is the dark of the moon (pure objectivity, where no life is possible); at the bottom is the full moon (pure subjectivity, and at this point in the cycle of the individual man the spirit may leave the body and encounter other spirits); on the opposite sides of the circle are the two quarters. Between the dark and the first quarter we have a primitive condition of violence and elementary learning, the struggle between the spirit and brutality. Between the first quarter and the full we aproach creativity, and between the full and the second quarter we depart from creativity. The period of the greatest creativity is on both sides of the full and close to it. Between the second quarter and the dark we are in the period of wisdom, in which creativity is almost at an end, and are approaching death, in the life of a man, and the end of an era in terms of the historical cycle. The gyres are most easily represented by Richard Ellman's diagram of the two equilateral triangles lying on their sides[3]: the short lines of these triangles should be very short in relation to the long lines, and the tip of each triangle should reach to the middle of the short line of the other. This design gives us a cross-section of the interpenetrating cones or gyres. At the points where the long lines intersect, we have the period corresponding to the full moon on the circle. The cones rotate in opposite directions, and one of them is winding the thread of life from the other: this procedure is perning or gyring. At the end of a two-thousand year cycle there is a sudden and violent reversal and the perning starts in the other direction.

In addition to Yeats's explicit ideas, there are certain consistent attitudes which should be mentioned. In his early work of the Celtic twilight period, he relied very heavily for his subjects on the figures of Irish legend: Oisin, Cuchulain, Conchobor, Dierdre, and others, and at this time and later he created a few such characters independently: Red Hanrahan, Michael Robartes, and Owen Aherne for examples. But Yeats needed heroes for his work, and he came more and more to need contemporary heroes. The result was his attempt to transform himself and his friends into legendary heroes. The most important of the friends were Lady Gregory, Major Robert Gregory, John Synge, Shawe-Taylor, and Hugh Lane; but there were others, among them Douglas Hyde. None of these people except Lady Gregory and John Synge would be known outside of Ireland today had Yeats not written about them, and Lady Gregory would be very little known. In fact Synge's reputation in the early part of the twentieth century was due at least as much to Yeats as to Synge, and his reputation has shrunken greatly. I can remember the time when Synge was the greatest dramatist in English except Shakespeare. There is no harm in praising one's friends, but when so much hyperbole is expended upon people of small importance, the discrepancy between the motive and the emotion becomes increasingly evident with time; there seems to be someting ridiculous about it. Maude Gonne was a special case, for Yeats was in love with her; but his equation of Maude Gonne with Dierdre, Helen of Troy, and Cathleen ni Houlihan partakes of his dramatization of himself. His concern with his uninteresting relatives and ancestors would seem to be part of the same dramatization.

II

I will turn to the principal poems related to the theory of the historical cycles. *Leda and the Swan* describes the rape of Leda by Zeus in the form of a swan, a rape which led to the birth of Helen, the destruction of Troy, and the disintegration of early Greek civilization. The rape introduced the next cycle of Greek civilization, which ended with the collapse of "Platonic tolerance," "Doric discipline," and ultimately the Roman Empire. *Two Songs from a Play* describe the end of the second Greek Cycle and the beginning of the Christian. *The Second Coming* prophesies the imminent end of the Christian cycle. Each of these works deals with violence, for every cycle begins and ends in violence. Yeats admires violence in general and has little use for Platonic tolerance, Doric discipline, or the civilization produced by Chritsianity. This fact is especially important when we come to read *The Second Coming*.

The account of the rape in the first eight lines of *Leda and the Swan* (p. 211) is very impressively done, but an account of a rape in itself has very limited possibilities in poetry. The important thing here is this: that the rape is committed on a mortal girl by Zeus. In the significance of this fact will reside the power or weakness of the whole poem. In the first portion of the sestet we are told that the swan has engendered the fall of Troy and the death of Agamemnon, but there is nothing about the historical cycles: this has to be read in from what we know of Yeats's theories—which are, after all, ridiculous. The greatest difficulties reside in the remainder of the sestet. "Did she put on his knowledge with his power?" The question implies that she *did* put on his power, but in what sense? She was quite simply overpowered or raped. She did not share his power, unless we understand a mystical union in the sexual act, which I think is implied. And what about his knowledge? Was this the knowledge of the fall of Troy and the death of Agamemnon? Was it the knowledge that a new cycle was about to begin (in spite of the fact that there is no reference to the cycles in the poem)? Or was it the omniscience of the god, resulting from the sexual union, a knowledge which would include the two other forms of knowledge? I suspect the last, but I would have difficulty in proving it. Next we have to consider "the brute blood of the air." The swan as such is a brute and flies through the air. Zeus may be thought of as living in the air and descending from the air. But Zeus as such was not a brute in Greek Mythology, and his animal disguises were disguises; nevertheless he often appeared in brute forms. The brute form here would appear to be connected with the identification of sexual union with the mystical experience. Satan, however, was referred to in the middle ages as the Prince of the Air, and he and his demons were said to live "in darkened air." I do not recollect that Yeats has mentioned this fact anywhere, but the fact is easily avail-

7

able, and it seems to me unlikely that Yeats would have overlooked it. Yeats was fascinated with the concept of demonic possession as a form of the mystical experience and with the possibility of obtaining supernatural knowledge from such possession. In *The Gift of Harun al-Rashid* (p. 439), the young wife is possessed by a Djinn, apparently as a result of sexual awakening, and in her sleep she communicates the k n o w l e d g e which her husband desires. This is a pretty fantasy, I suppose, but one can scarcely take it seriously. But we return to the question: is Zeus a god or a demon, or does it make no difference? It should make a difference if we are to adjust our emotions to the motive, for what is the motive? Then there is the difficulty that the poem ends with a question. A question, if it is really a question, is a weak way in which to end a poem, for it leaves the subject of the poem unjudged. But this question may be, as I suspect it is, a rhetorical question: in this event the answer should be either *yes* or *no*. There is nothing in the poem to help us choose, but from what I know of Yeats, I think that Yeats expected us to say *yes*. This brings us to the final difficulty: the vehicle of the poem is a Greek myth, and there is no harm in this if the tenor is serious; but the tenor is a myth of Yeats's private making, and it is foolish. That is, if we are to take the high rhetoric of the poem seriously, we must really believe that sexual union is a form of the mystical experience, that history proceeds in cycles of two thousand years each, and that the rape of Leda inaugurated a new cycle; or at least we must believe that many other people have believed these things and that such ideas have seriously affected human thinking and feeling. But no one save Yeats has ever believed these things, and we are not sure that Yeats really believed them. These constitute his private fairy tale, which he sometimes took seriously and sometimes did not. I see no way to make up one's mind about this poem except to decide that it is one of two things: an "aboli bibelot d'inanité sonore" or an "aboli bibelot de bêtise sonore." I feel sure that it is the latter, but I wish it were the former, for the former would at least be inscrutable and would call for greater skill on the part of the poet. The sonority is real, and I can appreciate it as well as the next man, but it takes more than sonority to make a great poem. Pure sonority eventually comes to seem pompous and empty.

Two Songs from a Play (p. 210) exhibit the same sonorous rhetoric and much of Yeats's private mythology: the difficulties therefore are similar to those in *Leda*, but there are certain passages which, as fragments, are effective. Mr. Unterecker (*A Reader's Guide*, p. 186) gives a page of explanation of the poem. He equates the fierce Virgin and her Star with Virgo and Spica (of the zodiac), with Astraea and the Golden Age, with the staring Virgin (Athena) and the heart of Dionysus; and he tells us that these anticipate respectively Mary and Christ, Mary and the Star of Bethlehem, Mary and the Christian Age, and Mary and Christ's heart. This is a sufficiently complicated set of relationships for a poem of sixteen lines in the course of which the relationships are not explained, but I suspect that there is one additional complication. In the poem entitled *A Nativity*, (p. 332) a poem in which the symbolic method is medieval, we have the line: "Another star has shot an ear"; and of this and other similar figures Yeats tells us: "I had in my memory Byzantine mosaic pictures of the Annunciation, which show a line drawn from a star to the ear of the Virgin. She conceived of the Word, and therefore through the ear a star fell and was born" (*A Reader's Guide*, p. 220). The fierce Virgin at the end of the first song is, of course, Mary; she must be fierce, because each new era begins in violence: we thus substitute Yeats's private myth of the Virgin for the traditional one. Similarly it was the odor of Christ's blood (in the second song) which put an end to Platonic tolerance and Doric discipline; that is to say, it was the violence of the new religion, the "Galilean turbulence" of Christ. The Babylonian starlight and the fabulous darkness indicate the same thing: we observe the starlight most clearly in the dark of the moon, which is the period of pure objectivity and of the violent reversal of the gyres. The rhetorical force in the poem is close to Yeats's best—but it is purely rhetorical. What he is saying is almost as foolish as what he says in section III of *The Tower* (p. 195), especially the twelve lines beginning "And I declare my faith." These lines are uttered with a passion which is obviously meant to be convincing, but who can be convinced? Unless we are convinced, the passion is meaningless. The second half of the second song is an excellent elegiac stanza, but it has only a loose connection with what has preceded.

The difficulties are similar in *The Second Coming* (p. 184). In line six, the expression "the ceremony of innocence" is misleading and awkward. By reading *A Prayer for My Daughter*, which follows, one discovers that the phrase means the ceremonious life in which innocence flourishes; but as one comes to it in the poem, it would seem to indicate some kind of ceremony, perhaps baptismal, perhaps sacrificial, perhaps some other. Otherwise the first eight lines are very impressive if one takes them phrase by phrase: the adjective *mere* in the fourth line, for example, is a stroke of genius. But what do the lines mean? One who has lived through the last thirty years and who has not observed the date of the poem (the volume was published in 1921) may feel that Yeats was writing about the growth of fascism, nazism, or communism:

> the worst
> Are full of passionate intensity.

But the first two are impossible and the third is unlikely. "The best" are the Irish aristocrats; "the worst" are the Irish engaged in politics, who were trying to establish a constitutional democracy and who eventually succeeded. The poem is an attack on civilized government made by a man who felt an intense dislike for democracy and the political activity without which democracy cannot survive—a dislike which was due in part to his native temperament but largely, I fear, to the fact that Maude Gonne was more interested in politics than in Yeats; by a man who, during much of his later life, was often tempted in the direction of fascism. The first four and a half lines of the second section are an example of Yeats's high rhetoric, but for their effect they depend upon our belief in his notion of the Spiritus Mundi. From there on we have his description of the beast, which is a fine description. But the account of the beast is not pure description. If we are to take it as seriously as Yeats's language indicates that we should, we must again accept his theory of the gyres as in some way valid. And if we do this, we must face the fact that Yeats's attitude toward the beast is different from ours: we may find the beast terrifying, but Yeats finds him satisfying—he is Yeats's judgment upon all that we regard as civilized. Yeats approves of this kind of brutality. When we consider all of these complications, it becomes very difficult to arrive at an acceptance of the poem, an acceptance both rational and emotional. I do not deny that civilization may be coming to an end— there is no way of knowing, although I think that the chances of its surviving for a long time are fairly good. But if we are to have a poem dealing with the end of civilization, and one that we can suppose to be great, the poem must be based on something more convincing than a home-made mythology and a loose assortment of untenable social attitudes. We need to invoke the Mallarméan concept of the symbol to save this poem, but we cannot invoke it because the ideas are perfectly clear,

III

I will next consider *Sailing to Byzantium* and *Byzantium*.

Sailing to Byzantium (p. 191) opens with a very good stanza. The first four lines of the next stanza are unfortunate. In the first two lines we have Yeats's routine figure of the scarecrow, a melodramatic characterization of his own old age, and one which becomes very tiresome. In the next two lines we have one of his melodramatic renderings of emotion through ridiculous physical action:

> unless
> Soul clap its hands and sing, etc.

The fact that this figure came from Blake does not help it. It is similar to other and earlier passages:

> Until I cried and trembled and rocked to and fro

from *The Cold Heaven* (p. 122), and:

> While up from my heart's root
> So great a sweetness flows
> I shake from head to foot

from *Friends* (p. 122). Both of these poems were published in *Responsibilities*, in 1914, when Yeats was approximately forty-four years old. The book preceding was published in 1910. These two poems, then, were written between the ages of forty and forty-four, when Yeats ought to have been too old for such immature pseudo-poetics, but actually this kind of thing went on for the rest of his life. The next four lines of the stanza are admirable, and the third stanza is one of the most impressive in Yeats except for the phrase: "perne in a gyre." To perne in a gyre means to take part in life: Yeats is inviting the sages who are now in eternity to return from eternity to life and become his teachers. The phrase, however, is bad in two ways: first, it gives us the images of the sages stepping from the wall and then spinning like tops or dervishes; second, it does not really mean this, but is a dead metaphor for the return to life. This is one of many examples of the use of medieval symbolism, which in Yeats amounts to a kind of personal shorthand, of unrealized figures of speech. An unrealized figure of speech, as I use the term, is one in which the vehicle or the descriptive matter is dead; in such a figure one has to deduce the tenor from the dead vehicle. It would better to use abstract language precisely. The last stanza is well written, but the view here given of the function of the poet (to say nothing of the portrait of God) is distressing: the poet, having achieved immortality, will sing to keep a drowsy emperor awake, and he will sing to lords and ladies who are, presumably, equally drowsy. This is the legendary function of the bard, a function which fascinated Yeats, a function which he seems to have tried to fulfill in the Gregory household. The stanza is no accident. We find much the same idea in an earlier piece, *On Being Asked for a War Poem* (p. 153):

I think it better that in times like these
A poet's mouth be silent, for in truth
We have no gift to set a statesman right;
He has had enough of meddling who can please
A young girl in the indolence of her youth,
Or an old man upon a winter's night.

One cannot object to Yeats's refusing to write a poem to order, on war or any subject; but the reason given is feeble and characteristic—it exhibits Yeat's sentimental and anti-intellectual view of the nature of his art. The final words of *Sailing to Byzantium,* "to come", do not in themselves indicate that the poet is in any sense a prophet (there is, of course, no reason why he should be, but this concept might seem to improve the poem), for he, like the Emperor and the lords and ladies, is now in eternity, and they all know what is to come. What is to come, like what is past or passing, merely provides material for this kind of poetry.

Byzantium (p. 243) has often been regarded as one of the most obscure of the poems, but the meaning is fairly obvious. As most of the commentators say, the poem deals with the poet looking out from eternity on those who are coming in; it thus differs from its companion piece, which deals with the poet's voyage to eternity. Curiously enough, although the city of Byzantium is eternity, it seems to be eternity only by night; by day it is corrupted by fury, mire, and blood—but this difficulty is not really great. The starlit or moonlit dome and the bird of the third stanza have led T. R. Henn (the only commentator, so far as I can recollect, who has risked explaining them) rather far from the Yeatsian system[4]. It seems to me unlikely that the bird is a male symbol and the moon a female. In the first stanza, a starlit dome is a dome in the dark of the moon, in the period of perfect objectivity or absolute death; a moonlit dome (in this stanza one is forced to suppose that the moon is the full moon) is a dome in the period of perfect subjectivity, when the spirit leaves the body. Either dome would thus disdain man in his essentially human periods. In the third stanza, the golden bird, like the golden bird of the other poem, is an eternal bird, a bird of absolute death; it is on a starlit golden bough and can crow like the cocks of Hades. The meaning of all this strikes me as perfectly clear, as clear as the meaning of any medieval symbol. Such a bird would be embittered by the moon because the moon marks the stages of human life; the two stanzas support this interpretation in all their details. The second stanza, which is an interruption of the argument conducted in one and three, and which would function more effectively as the third than as the second, gives us the poet's invocation of the dead, his attempt to become one with them. The fourth stanza deals with the purification of the entering spirits, and the fifth with their struggle to enter: as far as the mere logic of the discussion goes, these stanzas ought to be in reverse order. The order probably contributes as much as the esoteric symbols to the difficulty that many readers have found in the poem. The order may have been intentional—may have been an attempt to befuddle the reader into believing that medieval method was Mallarméan method—but after about forty years of reading Yeats, I believe that the order was accidental. As we have been told, the sea is doubtless a symbol for life, and the dolphins who carry the dead to Byzantium are incidentally phallic symbols: the sea is thus tormented by the phallic symbols and by the gongs, which are a call to death. We scarcely have the inpenetrable image here (Mallarmé was incomparably more skillful at that); we merely have excitement and carelessness. If we study Yeats's private system we can discover to a certainty what starlight means: its meaning is as definite as the meaning of Dante's panther. The trouble is that, like Dante's panther, it is merely a shorthand device for an idea. Star-

light tells us nothing about death; the panther tells us nothing about lust. In so far as either is described well at the sensory level, it is good decoration—but it is essentially decoration and does nothing to clarify the subject. Yeats's poem is almost wholly decoration, and the ornaments are drawn from his private myths. The generality of the meaning of the ornament drawn from such myths is essentially of the same kind as the generality of the cliché: it has nothing in common with the precise generalization of abstract terms. Yeats had, in fact, only a vague idea of what he was talking about. He did his talking in terms of sensory details, which everyone believes (in our time) to be essential to poetry. The fact that his details do not embody definite thought (as the sensory details of Stevens and Valéry often do) and the fact that his details are often poorly realized at the sensory level do not disturb his admirers, for his language is violent. We are in search of easy emotion, and we find it in Yeats.

IV

Among School Children (p. 212), like the poems which I have already discussed, is regarded as one of the greatest. The first stanza is quietly and effectively descriptive. The second stanza opens with one of his personal clichés, "a Ledaean body": the body is Ledaean because it is the body of Helen, daughter of Leda—that is to say, of Maude Gonne. But none of us have ever seen Leda or Helen, and in a few more years there will be no one who has ever seen Maude Gonne, and the portraits of Maude Gonne which I have seen are not very convincing. This is a somewhat pretentious way of saying "a

12

very beautiful body", but it is not description—it is easy allusion. What we have is an overtone from the Greek myth and from the Yeatsian myth, both very thin. Helen destroyed the civilization of her time and was thus heroic. Yeats believed that Maude Gonne was destroying the civilization of her time, and he longed to see it destroyed (although he regretted her personal part in the destruction). Therefore the two women were similar, not merely in their beauty but in their action. But Maude Gonne played a real, though minor, part in establishing a civilized government in Ireland, and her son Sean MacBride played his part also. If Maude Gonne was really heroic (I am not a specialist in Irish history nor an aficionado of the Irish temperament), it was in a way that Yeats was incompetent to understand. Maude Gonne was neither Helen nor Dierdre; she was a vigorous and practical (albeit Irish) woman. She may have been beautiful and she may have had faults and virtues which are irrelevant to this discussion, but Yeats did not understand what she was doing. As Mrs. Yeats is reported to have said, Yeats simply did not understand people. One can find additional testimony to the same effect in the letters of Ezra Pound—letters written when Pound was young and still a pretty shrewd observer. This may seem to be too much talk about a mere phrase: the point is that Yeats regularly employed mere phrases. Other clichés in these lines are "I dream" and "bent above a sinking fire." In the sixth line the sphere contains the idea in a general way, but not with the precision that would have been possible with abstract language or

a better figure; the egg adds nothing to the significance of the sphere and is comical in itself. The third stanza introduces fewer and less troublesome difficulties; but such phrases as "fit of grief or rage" and "daughters of the swan" are mechanical, and "my heart is driven wild" is stereotyped melodrama of a sort to which I have already objected and shall object again. The fourth stanza is composed almost wholly of similar clichés and concludes with Yeats's favorite, that of the scarecrow. Stanzas five and six are of much the same kind: shoddy diction, carelessly violent diction, and further exploitation of the scarecrow. The two lines about Plato are passable but scarcely profound; the two lines about Aristotle are ridiculous without being witty; the lines about Pythagoras mean nothing, except that they raise a curious question about the mechanics of fiddling, an art with which Pythagoras was not acquainted. The seventh stanza seems to be the beginning of an important statement, but unfortunately it is part of a statement which is continued in the final stanza. The final stanza is one which I can understand in terms of the pseudo-mysticism and anti-intellectualism of the past two hundred and fifty years, but I cannot grasp it imaginatively—that is, in terms of human life as I know human life. The word *labour* seems to mean fruitful labor, or ideal labor. But where does this kind of labor exist, except, perhaps, in the life of a tree? The body is always bruised to pleasure soul; wisdom is always born out of midnight oil or out of something comparable. The diction in these lines is abominable: the first two lines are bad enough, but the third and fourth are as bad as Keats's "Here where men sit and hear each other groan". The question addressed to the tree is preposterous: the tree is obviously more than the leaf, the blossom, or the bole, but these all exist and can be discussed, and it is because of this fact that we have words for them— the implication of the passage is that the tree is an inscrutable unit, like the Mallarméan poem. The diction of the seventh line is as bad as that of the third and fourth. The last line is similar to the fifth and sixth. When we watch the dancer we may not discriminate, although a choreographer could; but if the dancer and the dance could not be discriminated in fact the dancer could never have learned the dance. Precisely the same ideas will be found in Emerson's *Blight*, a small affair but somewhat better written.

V

I have had something to say of Yeats's habit of excessive dramatization. I would like to be a little more explicit on this subject and then proceed to a few of his poems on his friends and on his political attitudes. I will quote two of Yeats's very minor poems and compare them briefly with two poems by John Synge[5] on the same subjects. First is Yeats's poem *A Coat*: this is the last poem in *Responsibilities* and is his farewell to the style of the Celtic Twilight:

I made my song a coat
Covered with embroideries
Out of old mythologies
From heel to throat;
But the fools caught it,
Wore it in the world's eyes
As though they'd wrought it.

Song, let them take it,
For there's more enterprise
In walking naked.

As I have tried to show, Yeats never learned to walk naked, although he managed to shed a few of the more obvious ribbons of the eighteen-nineties. Here is Synge's poem:

The Passing of the Shee
After looking at one of A. E.'s pictures

Adieu, sweet Aengus, Meave, and Fand,
Ye plumed yet skinny Shee,
That poets played with hand in hand
To learn their ecstasy.
We'll stretch in Red Dan Sally's ditch,
And drink in Tubber Fair,
Or poach with Red Dan Philly's bitch
The badger and the hare.

I will now quote Yeats's poem (also from *Responsibilities*) *On Those That Hated 'The Playboy of the Western World'*:

Once, when midnight smote the air,
Eunuchs ran through Hell and met
On every crowded street to stare
Upon great Juan riding by:
Even like these to rail and sweat
Staring upon his sinewy thigh.

That slow, that meditative man himself wrote as follows:

The Curse
To a sister of an enemy of the author's who disapproved of "The Playboy."

Lord, confound this surly sister,
Blight her brow with blotch and blister,
Cramp her larynx, lung and liver,
In her guts a galling give her.

Let her live to earn her dinners
In Mountjoy with seedy sinners:
Lord, this judgment quickly bring,
And I'm your servant, J. M. Synge.

Yeat's poems are inflated; they are bardic in the worst sense. Synge's poems are witty and unpretentious. Synge was not, I think, a great dramatist, but he wrote a few

14

fine, though small, poems, of which these two are the best.

To a Friend Whose Work Has Come to Nothing (p. 107) exhibits the same inflated style and Yeats's predilection for madness. The first ten lines are plain and honest and exhibit a certain moral nobility; the last six, however, recommend madness as a cure for the problem propounded. We are told that the poem was addressed to Lady Gregory. Lady Gregory never followed the advice here given, but as she appears in this poem she is merely one in a long series of Yeatsian lunatics.

In Memory of Major Robert Gregory (p. 130) is a poem in praise of Lady Gregory's son, who was killed in the first world war. It is commonly described as one of the greatest poems in our language; I confess that I think it a very bad poem. The first two stanzas deal with Yeats's recent settling in his new house and with his thoughts about dead friends; the next three stanzas deal with three dead friends in particular: Lionel Johnson, John Synge, and Yeats's uncle, George Pollexfen; the next six stanzas deal with • Robert Gregory; the final stanza is a conclusion. The first stanza is quiet and acceptable, though undistinguished. The second stanza, undistinguished in general, contains two very awkward details: the third and fourth lines employ a conversational and verbose stereotype to embody a simple matter, and the fifth line employs another. The fifth line, however, is bad in other ways: the words *up upon* make a crude combination, and the whole line, "And quarrels are blown up upon that head", gives us, like the two lines preceding, a dead metaphor but this time a

mixed metaphor. Unless we are imperceptive of the possibilities of language, we visualize something being blown up on top of a head. This kind of thing is common in newspaper writing and in other vulgar writing. I remember a freshman composition from many years ago, in which the student wrote: "This line of study is basic to my field of endeavor." It is the same kind of thing, and no apologetic reference to the virtues of colloquialism is an adequate defense. The third stanza, which deals with Lionel Johnson, is stereotyped throughout, but it contains two especially unfortunate details. Johnson is described as "much falling", a sufficiently clumsy phrase in itself, but Pound tells us

"how Johnson (Lionel) died
By falling from a high stool in a pub ..."[6]

It seems likely that Pound's poem was written somewhat after that of Yeats, as far as I can judge from the dates at my disposal, and that the passage was intended as a comment on Yeats's phrase. At any rate, it is a fair enough comment. Immediately below "much falling" we get a very thin reincarnation of Roland's horn. The fourth stanza deals with John Synge. He is described as "that enquiring man," a phrase to which I do not object in itself. But every time Synge appears by name in Yeats's poems, he is described as "that . . . man", and we expect the formula as regularly as we come to expect rock, thorn trees, cold light, shaking and trembling, and scarecrows; furthermore the unnecessary use of the demonstrative adjective is one of Yeats's most obviously mechanical devices for achieving overemphasis. The remainder of this

15

stanza is undistinguished, but one should consider these details: in line five, *certain* is used as a pronoun instead of as an adjective; in line six we have "a most desolate and stony place"; and in the last we have "Passionate and simple like his heart", a phrase which is not only one of Yeats's common clichés but one which indicates as clearly as many others the anti-intellectual bent of his work. The fifth stanza deals with Yeats's uncle, George Pollexfen, who, it seems, had been a vigorous horseman in his youth, but who had devoted himself to astrology in his later years. The diction is dull, but once again there are strange details. For example, if solid men and pure-bred horses are determined by the stars, then why not other men and horses? The limitation, I suppose, could have been clarified by such a word as *even*, but the writing is slovenly: as Pound said long ago, poetry should be at least as well written as prose. The words *outrageous, sluggish,* and *contemplative* indicate that Yeats disapproved of his uncle's later interests because they were, in some sense, intellectual; but Yeats himself was interested, throughout much of his life, in equally pseudo-intellectual studies. Perhaps the stanza is what Cleanth Brooks would call ironic; but it is also dull. The sixth stanza is respectably executed except for two details. In the second line "as it were" says nothing; it may have been used to fill out the line and achieve a rime, or it may have been used in the interests of colloquial style, although it is not colloquial. It seems to be lazy. The next to the last line, "Our Sidney and our perfect man," is exorbitant praise. One might accept it as a mere outburst of grief except for the fact that Yeats devotes the rest of the poem to praising Gregory in these terms: he was a great horseman, scholar, and painter; he had the knowledge to give expert advice in architecture, sculpture, and most of the handicrafts. He may well have been a great horseman, but so is many a jockey; the praise in the other departments, however, appears excessive, for if it were not we should have heard of Gregory's accomplishments from o t h e r sources. He appears to have been no Sidney, but a charming and admirable young man who dabbled in the arts. We have familiar stereotypes in the last stanzas: cold rock and thorn, stern color, delicate line, secret discipline, none of them really described or defined; we have the facile commonplaces of the final lines of stanzas eight and nine and the somewhat comical example of misplaced particularity in the final line of stanza eleven. In stanza eleven the figure of the fires is a good example of the unrealized figure of speech: that is, the two fires tell us nothing about the two temperaments except that some people live rapidly and briefly, some slowly and longer, and at the descriptive level the fires are uninteresting. In the twelfth and final stanza, Yeats tells us that he had hoped in this poem to comment on everyone whom he had ever loved or admired but that Gregory's death took all his heart for speech. He had managed to write twelve stanzas of eight lines each, however, before he stopped; but this remark serves as a kind of apology for the loose structure of the poem—a structure which remains loose in spite of the apology.

Coole Park, 1929 (p. 238) is a

poem in honor of Lady Gregory and her home, Coole Park, which she had been forced to sell to the Forestry Department, though she was permitted to live there until her death. The poem is a typical meditation on the virtues of old families and their patronage of the arts, but especially upon Lady Gregory as a force in bringing distinguished men together and guiding their work. The theme is therefore the intellectual force that Lady Gregory exerted upon these men: Douglas Hyde, a negligible poet who became a distinguished Celtic scholar, whose poetry Yeats apparently admired and whose scholarship he regretted; John Synge, whose plays Yeats greatly admired and vastly over-rated; Shawe-Taylor and Hugh Lane, nephews of Lady Gregory and patrons of the arts but scarcely great men; and Yeats himself. Shawe-Taylor and Lane are described as "those impetuous men". This is a Yeatsian formula to describe distinguished gentlemen, and Synge appears in the usual formula for Synge: "that slow, that meditative man." The unfortunate Hyde is buried in the worst pseudo-poeticism of all, and Yeats employs a prettily apologetic description of himself. The central figure of speech appears in the third stanza. The first two lines of the first place Lady Gregory and a swallow together in what appears to be an accidental juxtaposition, but in the third stanza the men are compared to swallows, and we are told that Lady Gregory could keep a swallow to its first intent, could control the flight of swallows. Obviously she could do nothing of the sort; we may suppose that she could control talented men in some fashion, but we are not told how. The

movement of the swallows is charming; Lady Gregory's influence on the men, presumably an intellectual influence, is never given us. What we have is a fairly good vehicle with almost no tenor, or fairly good decoration of an undefined theme. In the last two lines, however, the third stanza collapses almost completely. Line seven reads: "The intellectual sweetness of those lines." At the level of the vehicle, the lines are those of the swallows' flight; at the level of the tenor, we have nothing, for "intellectual sweetness" is merely a sentimental phrase with no conceptual support. The last line of this stanza, "That cut through time or cross it withershins," is especially unclear. How did the line of the swallows, either as vehicle or as tenor, cut through time? As to *withershins*, the *Shorter Oxford English Dictionary* gives this account of it:

1. In a direction contrary to the usual; the wrong way—1721. 2. in a Direction contrary to the apparent course of the sun (considered as unlucky or causing disaster) —1545.

The last line of the first stanza is pseudo-poetic. The third and fourth lines of the last stanza are commonplace, and the sixth and seventh are baffling: why should the mourners stand with their backs to sun and shade alike, and why is the shade sensual? This is verbiage for the sake of verbiage.

The best poem of this kind, I believe, is a late one, *The Municipal Gallery Revisited* (p. 316). There are a good many characteristic defects. In his attempt to achieve a conversational tone (or perhaps out of inadvertence) Yeats wrote a fair number of lines which are awkward in movement. The poem is predominantly iambic pentameter, but if we are to read it in this meter, we encounter problems, some more serious than others. Line four can be read only as three trochees followed by two anapests. In line eight of the same stanza we get this:

A revolútionary sóldier knéeling tó be bléssed.

That is, we have four syllables in the first foot and either three or four in the second, depending on our pronunciation of *revolutionary*. It is hard to read the first line of the second stanza as anything but an alexandrine. In line three of the second stanza, we have a trochee in the last position if we pronounce Ireland correctly, but this is the only line in the poem where this awkward variation occurs, and we are not prepared for it and are tempted to mispronounce the word for the sake of the rime. Line five in the same stanza is an alexandrine and the first lines of four, five and six are alexandrines. We have such formulae as "terrible and gay" and "John Synge . . .that rooted man". At the opening of the fourth stanza we have rhetorical exaggeration:

Mancini's portrait of Augusta Gregory, 'Greatest since Rembrandt', oॉcording to John Synge;

But this is followed immediately by the almost weary qualification:

A great ebullient portrait, certainly.

At the opening of the third stanza we have the expression of emotion through physical action:

Heart-smitten with emotion I sink down,
My heart recovering with covered eyes.

But this is an account of an old old man looking at the portraits of his dead friends and is understandable, and it has not the empty violence of comparable passages from earlier poems. The transition from five to six is awkward. Yeats apparently thought that the line at the end of five needed a footnote, and I dare say it does; but he puts his footnote in parentheses at the beginning of six, and it is unimpressive as poetry, and it detracts from the unity of six. Except for this detail, six is well enough written, but its effect depends upon Yeats's view of the ideal society, "dream of the noble and the beggar-man," a view by which I find myself unmoved. The last stanza over-rates Yeats's friends, but is the moving statement of an old man who held them in high esteem and who now reviews them all in their official portraits, all of them being dead. Perhaps the best apology for this poem is to be found in a poem by Robert Bridges, written a good many years earlier, his *Elegy among the Tombs*:

Read the worn names of the forgotten dead,
Their pompous legends will no smile awake;
Even the vainglorious title o'er the head
Wins its pride pardon for its sorrow's sake;
And carven Loves scorn not their dusty prize,
Though fallen so far from tender sympathies.

The best of the political poems, I suspect, is *Easter* 1916. The worst fault in this poem is the refrain, "A terrible beauty is born." One can understand the sentiment, but the diction is pure Yeatsian fustian. In the first stanza I regret the repetition of "polite meaning-less words", but the defect, if it is a defect, is minor. In the line "To please a companion", however, we have an unrhythmical prose if we pronounce *companion* correctly; to save the rhythm, we have to say companee*un*. In the first seven lines of the next stanza, lines which are passably written, we have Yeats's view of what women should not do. In the next two lines,

This man had kept a school
And rode our winged horse.

we have a psuedo-poeticism, as bad as Hyde's sword or Roland's horn. A little farther on we have this:

So sensitive his nature seemed.

The line is written in a very rapid tetrameter, and it occurs in a poem which otherwise is written in heavily accented trimeter, and for the moment it ruins the movement. To save the meter, we should have to read *sens'tive*, but the *Shorter Oxford English Dictionary* does not give this pronunciation. In the third stanza, the stream and the other details of momentary change are the main part of the vehicle; the unchanging stone is the rest. The vehicle, as mere description, is very well handled. The tenor, however, is this: the truly spiritual life consists of momentary change; fixity of purpose turns one to an imperceptive stone. This is familiar romantic doctrine, but I see no reason to take it seriously. In the last stanza he tells us that the Easter Martyrs turned themselves to stones and perhaps in a poor cause, but he praises them for their heroism and laments their deaths. The poem is marred by certain faults of style and by more serious faults of thinking, which we must consider virtues if we are to be greatly moved by the poem.

VI

I will turn now to a few poems which seem to me the most nearly successful.

The Wild Swans at Coole (p. 129) is perhaps the best of these. The line "And now my heart is sore" is unfortunate, but otherwise the poem is excellently written. There are two unobtrusive but brilliant details which seem to permeate the entire poem. In the first stanza we are given a quiet but excellent description of the dry autumn at twilight. The fifth line reads: "Upon the brimming water among the stones." The word *brimming* separates the world of water from the world of dryness with an almost absolute precision, and this separation is the essence of the poem. In the fourth stanza we find a similar detail:

They paddle in the cold
Companiable streams . . .

The cold streams are companiable to the swans but not to the aging human observer. Richard Ellman gives us an interesting fact about the poem:

When this poem was first published in the *Little Review* in June 1917, the fifth and fourth stanzas were reversed. By putting the fourth stanza at the end Yeats made it possible to read it symbolically so that his awakening would be his death, a paradox well within his intellectual boundaries. Unfortunately, the word 'but' was now superfluous at the beginning of the last stanza; he nevertheless allowed it to remain.[7]

One could employ this incident to illustrate Yeats's carelessness, a carelessness which can easily be documented elsewhere; but the word is not superfluous. In the third line of the fourth stanza the swans are either on the water or in the air, and at the end of the stanza they are in the air. "But now," the last stanza tells us, they are on the water. This seems reasonable. And what is Mr. Ellmann's authority for believing that Yeats's awakening would be his death? If the authority is to be found in Yeats, I have never seen a citation of it. The question with which the poem ends would be troublesome if it could not be understood. Mr. Unterecker, a disarmingly naive seeker for richness of ambiguity, has this to say of it:

This complex question (and many others Yeats will soon be asking) suggests its own mysteries: like that of the swans the pattern of man survives; yet "I", awakening some day (into death?) will find the pattern of immortality "flown away" (and myself immortal?)[8]

Why should the swans be a pattern of immortality? Yeats implies clearly enough that they are an immortal pattern, but that is another matter. As Wordsworth said, "The Form remains, the Function never dies." Alice Meynell made this distinction between the poet (a mortal individual) and the birds (an immortal form) :

Hereditary song,
  Illyrian lark and Paduan nightingale,
Is yours, unchangeable the ages long;
  Assyria heard your tale;

Therefore you do not die.
  But single, local, lonely, mortal, new,
Unlike, and thus like all my race, am I,
  Preluding my adeiu.

The idea is easy to grasp, whatever one may think of the style. And why should Yeats's awakening signify Yeats's death? Let us remember that the poem was written when Yeats was nearing the age of fifty, and that he saw himself as a man of declining powers. His theories of the phases of the moon and of the gyres were merely a rationalization of opinions which he had long held, and the poem entitled *The Phases of the Moon* appeared in the same volume with our present poem. Yeats at this time is about to enter upon the fourth period, the period of "wisdom", in which creativity is lost; he is departing from subjectivity, which makes creation possible. The swan, moreover, has been traditionally a symbol for beauty, and in Yeats's system water and water birds represent subjectivity. I would judge, then, that in this poem Yeats sees in the swans a symbol of his poetic power, still present, but soon, perhaps, to be lost. The question then means: "On whom will this talent alight when it has left me?" The poem in these terms is clear and is a fine poem. The word *companionable*, as I have accounted for it, may seem to offer a difficulty if the talent is understood to be still present; but the talent seems to be on the point of departure, and the water (subjectivity), though companionable to the talent, is about to be uncompanionable to the poet.

I Am of Ireland (p. 262) appears to be a dialogue between Cathleen ni Houlinan (Maude Gonne) and W. B. Yeats. The lady seems to be inviting the poet to enter into Irish politics, and he finds the idea little to his liking. The poem is not a great poem, for the subject is too slight, but the movement and diction are masterly. Its chief weakness resides in the fact that it has to be paraphrased so baldly with reference to Yeats's life and prejudices. More information ought to be contained within the poem.

Long-legged Fly (p. 327) is one of the most interesting poems, but as usual there are difficulties. The first stanza describes Caesar planning a battle to save civilization, and the third stanza give us Michael Angelo painting the Pope's chapel, that is, creating civilization; but the second describes Helen practicing a tinker's shuffle on the empty streets of Troy. The refrain indicates that all three persons are engaged in deep thought over important action, but Helen is not depicted as thinking—she is depicted as unthinking; and although Helen brought about the fall of Troy, she did not plan the fall, but was merely an accidental cause. Although the detail of the second stanza is exceptionally fine, the theme collapses. Furthermore, in the opening lines of the third stanza, Yeats says that Michael Angelo is painting his Adam in order to provide a sexual awakening for girls at puberty (for documentation of this obsession see *Under Ben Bulben IV*—p. 341), and this strikes me as so trivial (and so wrong) an aim for the painter's work that the poem is badly damaged by it: it is an example of Yeats's pseudo-religious glorification of sexuality. Then there are the two versions of the refrain in the second stanza. In the edition which I am using the refrain at the end of the second stanza reads: *"His* mind". This cannot refer to Helen, and if it is correct, then we have some kind of supernal mind working through all three of the figures; this con-

cept would be very vague, and the first stanza, in this event, would be misleading. The editors of the Variorum edition, however, point out that this reading occurs only in my edition and they give "Her mind" as the correct reading. They are almost certainly right, but the bad proof-reading in almost all of Yeats's books would seem to indicate at least a possibility that they are wrong. If they are right, then the refrain at the end of the second stanza is meaningless. The descriptive details throughout the poem and the movement of the lines are about equally beautiful.

I would like to mention a few minor efforts for one reason or another. *For Anne Gregory* (p. 240) is a charming and witty poem. *Crazy Jane Grown Old Looks at the Dancers* (p. 255) is beautifully done as regards diction, syntax, rhythm, and the relation of syntax to the rhythm of both line and stanza. One can say, perhaps, that the subject is melodramatic, or, if not, that it is certainly of small importance. I admire the execution but seldom reread the poem. *Lullaby* (p. 259) is almost equally graceful and is equally slight. *After Long Silence* (p. 260) has often been highly praised. The first six lines are excellent, but at the end we are told that this is "The supreme theme of Art and Song":

> Bodily decrepitude is wisdom; young
> We loved each other and were ignorant.

This is not, of course, the supreme theme of art and song, but we ought to consider what the lines mean. Bodily decrepitude and wisdom (a contemptible quality, according to Yeats) are the same thing; both are reached in old age (in the fourth period of the moon). Youth, love, and ignorance are the best things in life according to the doctrine. Now I shall not speak in favor of bodily decrepitude, for I am beginning to experience it and know what it is; and I have nothing against youth and love, for I observe them about me daily and find them charming. But as a simple matter of fact, wisdom (in the normal sense of the word) is highly desirable and ignorance is not. In the world as it is, we cannot have everything at once, but we must take things as they come and pay for what we get. However, my interpretation of the sixth line may be wrong. Yeats may have meant that the two friends were discoursing upon the supreme theme for discourse; namely, Art and Song. In this event, the two final lines would mean: *faute de mieux*. Because of the syntax and punctuation, it is impossible to be sure, although the first of my two readings strikes me as the more likely; either way the detailed meaning of the two last lines is the same. *The Cat and the Moon* (p. 164) gives us a cat which is beautifully described and a moon which is merely a stage-property. *The Gyres* (p. 291) is very badly written: the first stanza in particular is pure Pistol. But the poem is also revealing, for Yeats is welcoming the destruction of civilization with enthusiasm, and is predicting the return of the kind of civilization which he admires and believes once to have existed. The reader of *The Second Coming* should study this poem as a companion-piece. The six poems entitled *Under Ben Bulben* (p. 341) give a clear summary of his ideas and attitudes, and are obviously offered as a final statement. One reads a succinct summary of the social ideas, for example, in the fifth of these, and of Yeats's attitude toward himself in the sixth. Mr. Unterecker believes that the horseman of the epitaph is one of the wild horseman of the mountains, who descend upon the world in times of disaster; this may be so, but I have always supposed him to be one of Yeats's ideal aristocrats. The wild horsemen appear in the first poem, the mortal horsemen in the fifth (as well as in *The Gyres*).

VII

First of all we should discard the idea that Yeats was in any real sense a Mallarméan symbolist. There is not, so far as my limited knowledge goes, any extensive translation of Mallarmé's criticism. The original prose is extremely difficult, and I do not believe that Yeats ever had a sufficient command of French to read it; he certainly had not in the years when he was forming his style. And Mallarmé's verse is more difficult than his prose[9]. The simple fact of the matter is, that Yeats (from *Responsibilities* onward at least, and often before) was usually trying to say something clearly. His obscurity results from his private symbols (mainly of the medieval variety), from the confusion of his thought, and from the frequent ineptitude of his style. From *Responsibilities* onward, in fact, he became more and more openly didactic. He quite obviously was deeply moved by his ideas and expected us to be moved by them. But unfortunately his ideas were contemptible. I do not wish to say that I believe that Yeats should be discarded, for there are a few minor poems which are successful or nearly successful, and there are many fine lines and passages in the more ambitious pieces. But in the long run it is impossible to believe that foolishness is greatness, and Yeats was not a great poet, nor was he by a wide margin the best poet of our time. There are greater poems in Bridges, Hardy, Robinson, and Stevens, to mention no others, and in half a dozen younger poets as well. His reputation is easily accounted for. In the first place there is real talent scattered through his work; in the second place our time does not recognize any relationship between thought and poetry, between motive and emotion; in the third place, Yeats's power of self-assertion, his bardic tone, overwhelmed his readers. The bardic tone is common in romantic poetry: it sometimes occurs in talented (but confused) poets such as Wordsworth, Blake and Yeats; more often it appears in poets of little or no talent, such as Shelley, Whitman, and Robinson Jeffers. For most readers the bardic tone is synonymous with greatness. If the poet asserts his own greatness long enough and in the same tone of voice the effect is hypnotic; we have seen the same thing on the political platform in such speakers as Adolf Hilter and Father Coughlin. But in time the effect wears off. While the tone is effective, however, a good deal of damage can be done and in fact is usually done. In our time Yeats has been regarded as the great poet in person, the poet of the impeccable style. He has thus become a standard of judgment for critics, with the result that the work of better poets has been obscured or minimized; and he has become a model for imitation, with the result that the work of a good many talented poets has been damaged beyond repair.

[1]*A Reader's Guide to William Butler Yeats*, by John Unterecker, the Noonday Press, New York, 1950.

[2]*Romantic Image*, by Frank Kermode, The Macmillan Co., New York, 1957.

[3]*Yeats: The Man and the Masks*, by Richard Ellmann, The Macmillan Co., 1948. P. 228.

[4]*The Lonely Tower*, by T. R. Henn, Methuen and Co. Ltd., London, 1950. P. 220.

[5]*Poems and Translations*, by J. M. Synge, John W. Luce and Company, Boston, 1911.

[6]*"Siena Mi Fe'; Disfescemi Maremma"* from *Hugh Selwyn Mauberly*.

[7]*The Identity of Yeats*, by Richard Ellman, Oxford University Press, 1954, p. 253.

[8]*A Reader's Guide*, p. 132.

[9]For an example, let me refer the reader to "literal" translations of *Tout Orgueil* by Fry and Fowlie respectively. Both men knew French thoroughly, and Fry was working with a Frenchman, Mauron. Both men were intelligent and conscientious students of the poet. The two versions of the sestet are essentially the same, but both are ungrammatical, and this fact ought to have put the translators on their guard, for Mallarmé is one of the most grammatical of poets, even though his syntax is seldom French. What we really have in the sestet is a suspended sentence, of which "le sépulcre" is the subject; this fact, plus the fact that the antecedent of "elle" follows the pronoun instead of preceding it, has thrown the translators off. The translation should go as follows (I translate the first three lines in reverse order for the purpose of clarifying the grammar): The sepulchre of disavowal/ gripping as if with claws/ the inevitable

agonies of the past/, (this sepulchre) under a heavy marble (slab) which it (i.e., the console) isolates/ is lit with no other fire/ than the glittering console. The console is not a table, but is an ornamental bracket supporting a marble mantel-piece. The fireplace is the sepulchre of disavowal because letters (I suppose) have been burned in it; it con- tains a claw-footed grate or claw-footed andirons. The poem describes a room in a deserted house. Ultimately this is one of many poems on ideal emptiness, or pure poetry. This kind of thing is as remote from Yeats's talent as it would have been from his understanding. Any obscurity in Yeats is a simple-minded obscurity.